Isabella Marchini Piva
Marco Antônio Rossi

The Wayfinding Process for People with Visual Impairments

Isabella Marchini Piva
Marco Antônio Rossi

The Wayfinding Process for People with Visual Impairments

A case study

ScienciaScripts

Imprint

Any brand names and product names mentioned in this book are subject to trademark, brand or patent protection and are trademarks or registered trademarks of their respective holders. The use of brand names, product names, common names, trade names, product descriptions etc. even without a particular marking in this work is in no way to be construed to mean that such names may be regarded as unrestricted in respect of trademark and brand protection legislation and could thus be used by anyone.

Cover image: www.ingimage.com

This book is a translation from the original published under ISBN 978-613-9-74359-9.

Publisher:
Sciencia Scripts
is a trademark of
Dodo Books Indian Ocean Ltd. and OmniScriptum S.R.L publishing group

120 High Road, East Finchley, London, N2 9ED, United Kingdom
Str. Armeneasca 28/1, office 1, Chisinau MD-2012, Republic of Moldova, Europe

ISBN: 978-620-6-28219-8

Copyright © Isabella Marchini Piva, Marco Antônio Rossi
Copyright © 2023 Dodo Books Indian Ocean Ltd. and OmniScriptum S.R.L publishing group

SUMMARY

CHAPTER 1	3
CHAPTER 2	7
CHAPTER 3	10
CHAPTER 4	27
CHAPTER 5	29

SUMMARY

This study aimed to analyse the General Library of UNESP / Bauru - SP, where the physical structure serves only people without visual impairments, in order to make a restructuring to adapt the physical space to the entire faculty and student body, including the visually impaired present. This research was carried out based on questionnaires that were applied to people with some type of visual impairment and / or people who deal daily with these. The themes involved: the greatest difficulties of mobility and localisation, environment and surroundings in the library, so that it was possible to identify the problems and readjust the environment to ensure inclusion. As for the structure, it was necessary to design spaces adapted to the needs of visually impaired users, respecting their sensory abilities and limitations. To this end, spatial planning and communication were important aspects to facilitate the *wayfinding* process.

Key words: *Wayfmding,* architectural projects, visually impaired.

CHAPTER 1

INTRODUCTION

1.1 ACCESSIBILITY

At the "World Conference on Education for All", held in Thailand in 1990, with the aim of rethinking the global situation of education, a document was drawn up that committed to guaranteeing quality basic education for all citizens, without exception.
(see:< https://www.unicef.org/brazil/pt/resources_10230.htm>). Thus, highlighting article 3° of this declaration, which signals the differentiated learning needs of the disabled, it is possible to verify the obligation of equal access to education for people with any type of disability. This research addressed visual impairment, which can be aggravated by the environment and dependent on the situation in which the user finds himself, that is, the more difficult the situation, the greater the degree of disability.

Thus, the inclusion of the disabled has required major challenges from the school, which does not always have an appropriate structure to carry out inclusion properly, as pointed out by the National Curriculum Parameters (PCNs) for special education (BRASIL, 1998).

However, knowing that school is a priority for any citizen of the world, it is the duty of the government to provide the necessary social support. Thus, with the collaboration of the school and the student himself, the combination of these three points, that is, government, school and student, makes it possible to improve to achieve efficiency from an interactivity.

According to Dischinger (2000), it is mainly through information and mobility that the individual participates in places and activities and establishes contact with other people, that is, exercising their right of citizenship and going to school is one of the essential activities of every citizen. However, it is common for people with visual impairments to prefer to be limited to certain physical spaces, being restricted from their right to come and go, due to the lack of information on the orientation of places. (LIMA, 2004). Not only, but also for this same reason, some disabled people feel embarrassed to move around in public environments, due to the greater chances of risks to which they are subjected, such as: falls, accidents, spatial disorientation or even stress. Consequence of this: negative influence of the environment on the spatial autonomy, social and professional life of the disabled person.

Some school environments are not built to meet the needs of the visually impaired, and the science of ergonomics is a possibility to improve the aspects already built and make the visually impaired feel safer in relation to the space, the environment. The case study, the General Library of the Universidade Estadual Paulista - UNESP, campus of Bauru, will be punctuated some questions about *wayfinding*[1] of libraries, that is, its structure and disposition, in order to favour and facilitate the issue of accessibility to perceptible information, so that the disabled can orient themselves calmly.

For Bins Elly (2002), orientation is a cognitive process that involves the individual's ability or capacity to mentally situate and/or move in a given physical space, and depends both on the information contained in the environment and on the individual's ability to perceive and treat this information. Following this line, the phenomenon of orientation is a process of knowing where one is, where to go beyond the act of moving, so it considers two basic levels that interact: spatial orientation as an abstraction phenomenon and spatial orientation as an operational dynamic phenomenon linked to the movement of the individual, that is, *wayfinding*.

Cognitive mapping is integral to information processing. It is relevant to present the distinction they make between cognitive map (tactile map) and cognitive mapping to understand *wayfinding* behaviour. Cognitive map is the mental image or representation of the configuration spaces of an environment. Cognitive mapping is the process in the structure of the mind, which provides the creation of the cognitive map (PASSINI & PROULX, 1988).

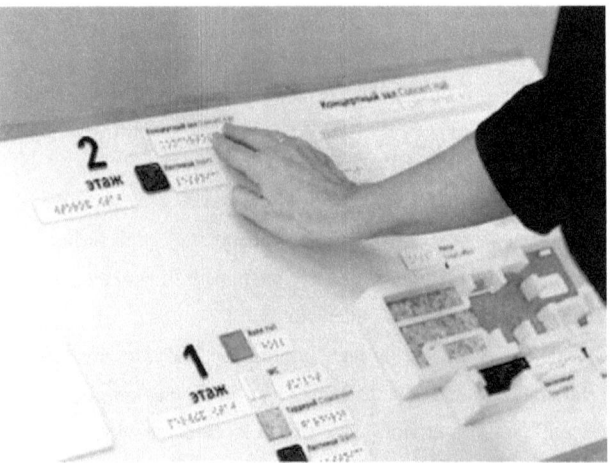

Fig. 1 - Tactile Map. Source: Maria Nikerman and Katerina Churakova.

It is known that the cognitive map of the visually impaired person is different from that of the one who sees, because he has visual images of spaces. The spatial experience of those who do not see comes from hearing, touch and movement (UNGAR, 2000).

According to the statement of Vygotsky (2000) in which the relationship of man with the world is mediated by instruments and signs, in the specific case of visual impairment, knowledge is mediated basically by the auditory/phonatory system and by the haptic/active touch system, which a tactile map is essential for the functioning of the place, in this case the library, so that the visually impaired can access books and articles without difficulty.

Fig. 3 - Tactile signage. Source: Maria Nikerman and Katerina Churakova.

In addition, working environments are subject to compliance with ergonomic standards. From 23 November 1990, through Law 6.514 Regulatory Standard n^0 17, Ergonomics (NR 17), of the Ministry of Labour and Employment (see: <http://www.guiatrabalhista.com.br/legislacao/nr/nr17.htm>). The standardisation for ergonomic issues was instituted in Brazil with the objective of NR 17, according to its section 17.1, is the establishment of a set of specifications to adapt working conditions to the psychological and physical characteristics of the citizen.

In this context, this research aimed to present contributions on informational accessibility, based on perceptible information, in order to restructure libraries by assisting the orientation process of visually impaired people.

1.2   BACKGROUND

The aim of this study was to improve access to the UNESP Library on the university campus in the city of Bauru - SP for people with disabilities or visual difficulties. Restructuring and adapting so that it is possible for the user to practice the exercise of citizenship safely. That is, the right to come and go, access to education, providing social integration and professional training.

1.3   OBJECTIVE

The objective of this research was to analyse the General Library of UNESP / Bauru - SP, where the physical structure serves only people without visual impairments, requiring a restructuring to suit the entire teaching and student body, including the current and possible future visually impaired. Thus, presenting some improvements that can be put into practice, within the analysed sector, designing the ergonomically correct workstation, providing adequate conditions so that partially and/or totally blind people can also perform activities with ease and safety.

CHAPTER 2

MATERIAL AND METHOD

2.1. ANALYSING DIFFICULTIES

This study was carried out by means of empirical research, i.e. producing and analysing data, always processing through empirical and factual control (Demo, 2000, p. 21). This research was based on two questionnaires, due to the analysis of different situations, in which the first involved an organisation that works directly with the teaching of visually impaired people; and the second the analysis of access to the library.

Thus, the questionnaires were applied emphasising the themes: the greatest difficulties of mobility and location, environment and surroundings in the library, so that the problems could be identified and the environment readjusted to ensure inclusion.

2.1.2 Questionnaire to the NGO AVISTAR (blind people of Piracicaba)

1- Do visually impaired people have access to reading? Do they have encouragement? If so, in what way?

2- Do they use the library? If yes, do they encounter any difficulties or would they like any improvements; if no, why?

3- Do disabled people have difficulty accessing the library?

4- Do they have a system for learning to read Braille? If yes, which one and how does it work? If not, do they have any projects in mind for this?

2.1.3 . Questionnaire to the Bauru Library

1- Are there any visually impaired users of the Library? If yes, do they find any difficulty in finding books through the computer? If not, do you think there is a lack of structure for their use?

2- Is there a collection in Braille? If not, how would you meet the needs of a disabled person if they need it, since it is their right?

3- What do you think most prevents disabled people from using the library?

4- Are there any suggestions for improvement that you would like to implement in the Library?

It was necessary to analyse *in loco in* order to have an even more precise assessment, so an interview was conducted with a mother and her son (DV), who is visually impaired and who attended the vestibular process in 2014. The interview aimed to understand the difficulties for the disabled to enter colleges, in addition to the previous trajectory throughout the schools. How was the support and support, also social inclusion, among other difficulties based on the school path.

As for the structure, it became necessary to design spaces adapted to the needs of the visually impaired user respecting their sensory abilities and limitations. To this end, spatial planning and communication were important aspects to facilitate the *wayfinding* process.

The concept of environmental graphic design then emerges: the process of designing to make social space more legible and inclusive, using strategies to develop guidance systems.

Accessibility to environmental information - proposed by NBR 9050 (2004), and by the principle of the tactile map - through sensory, verbal, tactile and pictorial communication through shapes, colours, textures, sounds, symbols and signs expressed in each space - exploring better to inform the user about it, exalting its characteristics and constituent elements.

Knowing that the process of identification and assimilation of the place is directly linked to the individual experience of users and their intellectual capacity, the latter was taken as a way that principles of space construction, such as spatial configuration, the presence or absence of referential elements, or functional zoning, act as "reading keys" of an environment, and can act to facilitate or hinder the understanding of space.

Several authors such as Bins Ely, Scariot, Passini, emphasise that a *wayfmding* information system can be formed through architectural information through the five primary elements (according to those identified by Lynch, 1997):

- Paths/circulation - people use them to develop their cognitive map of the place;
- Landmarks - object that identifies a locality, giving an identity to each part of the environment, they act as mental reference points;
- We - architectural and graphical information to help users make those decisions at the points that generate subsidiary parts;
- Boundaries - which determine where an area begins and where it ends;
- Zones/districts - areas with specific characteristics that aid general site identification.

For the environment in general, it is possible to implement floors, in high relief. With this type of flooring, blind people can identify that they are entering a different area from the one they are in at the moment. A good example are the branches of Banco Real: all of them have laid a special floor on the pavement, with grooves and high relief, which enters the bank and leads to all the strategic points (cashiers, electronic terminals, managers, among others). Each time a particular location is approached, the floor changes texture and the disabled person can guide themselves by cane or simply by the touch of their feet.

Another architectural application to explore is the use of odour dispersers. These are small, presence-sensing devices that give off a specific odour each time someone enters the room. A distinct smell is used for each room in the home, sharpening the sense of smell for recognition and localisation.

Initiating knowledge through sensory stimuli increases the ability of visually impaired people to understand and adapt to the subjects that will be taught. Exploring graphic materials, textures, type of printing, combined with Braille[2], can help in the education of blind and visually impaired individuals.

CHAPTER 3

DEVELOPMENT

We can define physical disability as "different motor conditions that affect people compromising mobility, general motor coordination and speech, as a result of neurological, neuromuscular, orthopaedic injuries, or congenital or acquired malformations" (MEC, 2004). According to Decree 3.956 (2001), disability is understood as: "a physical, mental or sensory restriction of a permanent or transitory nature, which limits the ability to perform one or more essential activities of daily living, caused or aggravated by the economic and social environment". According to Decree No. 5.296 of 2 December 2004, physical disability is : "complete or partial alteration of one or more segments of the human body, entailing impairment of physical function, presenting itself in the form of paraplegia, paraparesis, monoplegia, monoparesis, tetraplegia, tetraparesis, triplegia, triparesis, hemiplegia, hemiparesis, ostomy, amputation or absence of limb, cerebral palsy, dwarfism, limbs with congenital or acquired deformity, except aesthetic deformities and those that do not produce difficulties for the performance of functions". In this case, we are dealing with visual physical disability.

Among the information available in Brazil on the inclusion of the disabled, we highlight the work of Amaral (1995 and 1997), which presents a historical journey on the representations of disability, and the work of Mazzota (1993 and 1996), which succinctly portrays social attitudes underlying the treatment given to people with disabilities.

Taking into account the studies of Mazzota (1996), they point out three social attitudes that marked the history of Special Education in the treatment given to people with disabilities: marginalisation, welfarism and education/rehabilitation. Marginalisation is characterised as an attitude of disbelief in the possibility of change for people with disabilities, which leads to a complete omission of society in relation to the organisation of services for this population. Welfare is an attitude marked by a philanthropic, paternalistic and humanitarian sense, because there remains disbelief in the individual's ability to change, accompanied by the Christian principle of human solidarity, which seeks only to provide protection for people with disabilities. Education/rehabilitation is presented as an attitude of belief in the possibility of change for people with disabilities and the actions resulting from this attitude are directed towards the organisation of educational services. It should be emphasised that the fact that a social conception or attitude predominates in a given period does not mean that different conceptions and attitudes do not coexist in the same context.

In the 1970s, with the emergence of the integration proposal, students with disabilities began to attend ordinary classes. The advance of studies in the fields of psychology and pedagogy began to demonstrate the educational possibilities of these students. The attitude of education/rehabilitation prevailed as a new educational paradigm. However, there was also an attitude of marginalisation on the part of the educational systems, which did not offer the necessary conditions for students with disabilities to achieve success in regular school. According to Mrech (1998), the proposal for Inclusive Education emerged in the United States in 1975, with public law No. 94,142, which opened up possibilities for students with disabilities to enter regular school. Students with disabilities were included in this plan and won the right to study in regular schools. In this perspective, North American Inclusive Education, as well as that of other countries, such as Brazil, was limited only to the physical insertion of these students in the common education network, along the lines of the integration movement. Students were only considered integrated when they were able to adapt to the common class, as it was presented, without any adjustments to the already established educational system. Once again, the coexistence of educational/rehabilitation and marginalisation attitudes in the same educational context can be seen.

In the 1980s and 1990s, the proposal for the inclusion of students with special educational needs began, in an innovative perspective in relation to the integration proposal of the 1970s, whose results did not change much the educational reality of failure of these students. The inclusion proposal proposes that educational systems become responsible for creating conditions to promote quality education for all and make adjustments that meet the special educational needs of students with disabilities. Sassaki (1998, p.9) explains the inclusion paradigm: This paradigm is that of social inclusion - schools (both ordinary and special) need to be restructured to accommodate the full spectrum of human diversity represented by potential students, i.e. people with physical, mental, sensory or multiple disabilities and with any degree of severity of these disabilities, people without disabilities and people with other atypical characteristics, etc. It is the educational system adapting to the needs of its students (inclusive schools) rather than the students adapting to the educational system (integrated schools). Inclusive education therefore opposes the homogenisation of pupils according to criteria that do not respect human diversity. According to the Salamanca Declaration, in order to promote Inclusive Education, educational systems must assume that "human differences are normal and that learning should be adapted to the needs of children rather than to preconceived assumptions about the pace and nature of the learning process" (BRASIL, 1994, p. 4).

In the midst of inclusion and adaptation, for the visually impaired, we have that localisation and being localised depend on the concept of *wayfmding* and its application in the environment.

Fig.1 - visualisation of wayfinding. Source: photographer Aleks Yanchenkov.

When faced with an unfamiliar environment, with no idea of the space in advance, it is not possible for visually impaired people to make autonomous decisions to orientate themselves, plan and execute a route even with the help of a cane or a guide dog. First and foremost, anyone needs to know where they are in order to plan a route.

In this way, we enter a new specialised area, integrating more information and concepts to structure the way of localisation for the integration of the visually impaired.

We are dealing with graphic design and cognitive ergonomics, which, Padovani and Moura (2008) report the importance of the cognitive map for the *wayfinding* process, being a mental representation of the user's imagination together with its spatial organisation of the relationships of the elements (such as routes, distances, etc.) present in the spatial environment in question. The authors add that this representation can be built through direct interaction with the environment or by consulting external representations.

Fig. 2 - Environmental graphic design. Source: *Typography Heaven*.

In anthropology, the discussion on human spatial orientation, more specifically the cognitive process of *wayfinding*, has been carried out in the last two decades, according to Istomin and Dwyer (2009), under the aspects of theories such as "Mental Maps". This theory, according to Istomin and Dwyer (2009) is based on findings from disciplines such as social psychology and geography, and then adopted by British anthropologist Alfred Gell (1985) in that it assumes that: "*Wayfinding* is carried out in the light of spatial information stored in the form of a 'mental map' of the terrain, plus presumably some inferential schemata for converting this information into appropriate practical decisions and actions." (GELL, 1985. p.272) In geography, according to Raubal et al. (1997), for the process of spatial orientation or *wayfinding to* occur successfully, people need to have various cognitive abilities (such as object recognition) and also spatial knowledge. In relation to this, psychologists Siegel and White (1975) state that spatial knowledge is elaborated at the levels of action in space, perception of space and conception about space, all presented in an integrated way. The authors add that the construction of spatial representation is realised from the learning/knowledge of:

• landmarks (as a perceptual event, linked to the particularities of each place, as a recognition of the context);

• of routes (as a sensorimotor event, relating to specific paths for travelling from one point to another, as an association of changes from landmarks) and;

• configuration, also called survey (metric information on the relative location and estimated distance between landmarks, such as the interconnection of routes in a network as a whole). It can be seen from the above that the convergence of approaches to the *orientation/wayfinding* process is based on cognitive maps. This demonstrates the relevance of knowledge about their conformation for understanding how the user can perceive space and act in space.

It is considered that in the *wayfinding* process, the understanding of the environment (orientation) for the displacement action itself (navigation), according to Padovani and Moura (2008), has some aids such as: location indicators, circulation, emergency signalling, architecture, landmarks etc. Some of these aids can be materialised in visual artefacts which should be designed based on graphic design principles, more specifically information design. Visual artefacts provide the information necessary for spatial orientation, such as signs and signposts. These artefacts are physical supports mentioned by Bins Ely (2004), through which information is transmitted graphically. According to the author, these supports may be allocated in a space (such as signs, maps, banners) or be of individual use (such as leaflets, brochures, etc.), transmitting information by alphabetic or pictorial signs (BINS ELY, 2004, p.29). Technology also allows this information to be materialised in digital devices (totems, displays, Global Position System-GPS, smartphones, etc.). With this, it is perceived that signalling, an integral part of a *wayfinding* system, would be a set of graphic solutions applied in visual artefacts to direct/guide the user in the *wayfinding* process.

Returning to the field of Design, new specialisations have emerged in response to the enormous cultural and economic changes in our society. It can be said that Graphic Design, which works by providing information to the user, whether through language, image or symbols, has unfolded in several ways in the period between the end of the 20th century and the beginning of the 21st. One of these concerns the transmission of messages and information through the built environment. These are multiple layers of communication that help shape our understanding and sense of place (BEDROSSIAN, 2008). It is interesting to note that the boundaries between disciplines that interfere with space - architecture and design - have started to merge. In this context, architecture works with the conception of space and design with the provision of information (HUNT, 2003). This fusion came to be called later Environmental Graphic Design which, with its unique set of skills, helps us to read the world.

In its current configuration, the work of Environmental Graphic Design is found in three-dimensional environments such as cities themselves, mass transport systems, hospital complexes, cultural, educational and sports centres, and retail shops, for example. It includes signage, which when well designed is recognised as a major contributor to increased well-being and safety; ambience, which is important for its ability to create a sense of place for a given space and its power to reinforce a brand image; and exhibition design, which works with interpretive information by narrating or telling a story from a concept or theme to a company and its products.

Fig. 3 - Tactile flooring as a means of safe and efficient orientation and wayfinding for visually impaired people.
Source: Maria Nikerman and Katerina Churakova.

In this scenario, SEGD (*Society for Environmental Graphic Design*) works with the term Environmental Graphic Design. ADG (Association of Graphic Designers), on the other hand, works with this aspect only as environmental design, dividing it into two categories: signalling and ambience, also called total design. Combining the terminologies, the one adopted in this work - Environmental Graphic Design - is close to the one used in English *Environmental Graphic Design*. Even though the word environmental is often linked to ecological issues, the use of this nomenclature is defended because it is the closest to the desired practical sense. It is emphasised that environment is understood here as the surroundings of an individual, as Gibson defines: "[...] the essence of an environment is the surroundings of an individual" (1986, p. 43). This is not conformed by tactile limits, such as walls, but established by the observer during the process of reading and interpreting the codes present in the language. From this perspective, according to Jacob (2007), the notion of information is not separated from the notion of environment and is conceived as a unity.

It can be articulated, then, that the area of signalling and orientation works with design strategies that direct, inform and identify spaces. The area of ambience creates and shapes places and environments. And the area of exhibition design, in turn, educates and interprets information.

3.1 PRODUCT OF THE QUESTIONNAIRES

The first questionnaire was applied to analyse the difficulties of people with visual impairment and an NGO (AVISTAR) for the blind in Piracicaba. Below are the answers:

Question	Yes	No	Comment
Do visually impaired people have access to reading? Do they have incentives?	X		Resources for easy reading. Low vision: such as magnifiers, inclined plane, magnifying glasses. Blind people: Braille system. Within the institution, the pedagogue always encourages reading, both for adults and children, during and outside the sessions.
Do they use the library?		X	Most users do not use it because they find it too difficult to read Braille.
Do disabled people have difficulty accessing the library?		X	
Do they have a system for learning to read Braille?	X		All users are encouraged to learn the Braille system; children are compulsorily taught, within their school learning level; adults choose whether or not to learn Braille.

The second questionnaire was applied to analyse the difficulties faced by visually impaired people in the Unesp Library in Bauru itself. Below are the answers:

Question	Yes	No	Comment
Are there any visually impaired users of the Library? Do they encounter any difficulties?	X		There is a postgraduate student with low vision, but she does not use the resources available in the library, as the resources of her own personal computer are sufficient for her to have autonomy in her readings. In Bauru there are several equipment to assist, such as: screen reader software, character enlarger equipment, Braille line, scanner.
Is there a collection in Braille? How would you meet the needs of a disabled person?		X	Investment was made in equipment where visually impaired users can access *scanned* documents transformed into audios or use the Braille line where they can read through the Braille system itself; in addition, they take up a lot of physical space.
What do you think most prevents disabled people from using the library?			The physical limitation of the building itself, with difficulties of physical access and the historical difficulties on serious policies that include discussions related to people with disabilities on the agenda.
Are there any suggestions for	X		I believe that a joint work with students and teachers to better publicise the Library would be interesting,

improvement that you would like to implement in the Library?		since it is open to the public.

3.2 PRODUCT OF THE FIELD RESEARCH

A fieldwork was carried out to analyse and identify the accessibility of the Municipal library of Piracicaba and the library of UNESP Bauru. The field research was conducted in order to analyse the libraries:

a) Piracicaba Municipal Library

Fig 1- Book cover. Source: Author's own.

Fig 2- circulation without signalling. Source: Own author.

Fig 3- Lack of identification in books. Source: Own author.

Fig 4 - Braille collection of the Piracicaba Library, thick books, lack of identification on the sides and on the shelves.
Source: Own author.

b) Unesp Library in Bauru

Fig 5- Tactile Map located at the entrance of the Library. Source: Own author.

Fig 6- SIAI support. Source: Own author.

Fig 7- Document scanner to transform into audio. Source: Own author.

Fig 8- Tactile floor locator, used as a guide. Source: Author's own.

Fig 9- Tactile localiser guide to the area intended for DV, with the necessary equipment. Source: Own author.

From the theoretical basis, the answers to the questionnaires and the structural analysis of the libraries, it was possible to verify that access to it is not limited; that is, in the case of the UNESP Library in Bauru, it presents the main basic requirements of installation, location, structure and ergometry necessary to meet the needs of the visually impaired. However, there is no collection in Braille, so that if a book of this type is requested, it is necessary to send a letter to Unesp de Marília to have it printed there, since only on this Campus is there a large Braille printer.

Despite the aid equipment, their access is restricted, but for reasons of each person's own vision difficulty, such as complaints that the Braille book is not practical, due to its size, weight and takes more time to read the same as a person with vision without any alteration.

Thus, even with the incentives to read these people, the existing mechanisms for the practice are very exhaustive, and inefficient for the day-to-day, so that a book becomes much more pleasurable when made from the aid of book readers or audio computers. Thus, the use of the library, despite offering the same equipment, does not offer the comfort, since most users have such instruments and use them in their own home; nor environment for the use of audios.

In addition to these general reasons for any library, in the case of the university library, more specifically, the UNESP Library of Bauru, there is no visually impaired user. This is because there is currently no blind student.

Article 27 of Decree 3.298, of 20 December 1999, states: "Higher education institutions must offer adaptations of tests and the necessary support, previously requested by the student with a disability, including additional time to take the tests, according to the characteristics of the disability."

This decree aims to ensure that all candidates for a place at a university (private or private) have the same conditions to take the entrance exam. People with special needs (physical or otherwise) can and should be integrated into the society in which they live and have the right to study and practise a profession that suits them.

At UNICAMP (State University of Campinas), for example, the tests that need adaptation are made by the Centre for Studies and Research in Rehabilitation. Already at the entrance, candidates receive specialised assistance from psychologists, doctors, physiotherapists and even interpreters of Libras (Brazilian Sign Language).

All cases of disabled people who need special conditions to take the exams must be passed on to the entrance exam committee at the time of enrolment, however, cases of accidents that occur between enrolment and the date of the exam may be safeguarded by this law. After registering, a candidate for UERJ (Rio de Janeiro State University) had to undergo heart surgery and was hospitalised, but still managed to take the exam in hospital. Cases like this need to be communicated to the commission through a request attached to a medical report that proves the candidate's situation.

Visually impaired people are perfectly able to take part in the competitions. Those with impaired vision can request tests with enlarged letters or the aid of a magnifying glass. For those who cannot see at all, the exams can be written in Braille or the candidates can request the help of trained readers. In Rio de Janeiro, these candidates take their exams at a specialised centre: the Benjamin Constant Institute, located in Urca.

Candidates with dyslexia are entitled to take the test in a separate room with the help of a trained professional who reads the questions and transcribes the answers, all with extra time. The same goes for candidates with cerebral palsy or motor difficulties. Wheelchair users take their exams as close as possible to their home and always in ground-floor rooms. Some universities, such as the Federal University of Santa Catarina (UFSC), offer tests in Libras for deaf candidates.

According to INEP (National Institute for Educational Studies and Research Anísio Teixeira), the number of people with special needs in universities rose 179% between 2002 and 2007. In order to guarantee the inclusion of this group in universities, the Federal Public Prosecutor's Office of São Paulo has asked the Ministry of Education to only authorise and recognise higher education courses that offer full accessibility conditions, eliminating any type of physical barrier.

Although all entrance exams are required by law and offer means for disabled people to take the tests, according to data from the 2005 Higher Education Census prepared by the National Institute for Educational Institutional Studies and Research Anísio Teixeira (Inep), enrolment of people with disabilities was 6,022 nationwide, which represents an extremely low number of entries. (AUMENTA, 2018)

The reason is not related to the difficulties in carrying out the entrance exams, since right in the registration of the exam there is a gap for if you have a disability and an attachment for the certificate of the same. Once you have registered, the Teaching Commission will contact you by e-mail to ask you what you need to do the exam, such as extra time, equipment, a companion, among others.

One of the obstacles to increased inclusion is the disability itself, since it makes it extremely difficult to perform some professions, such as doctor, dentist, architect, among others that depend on a precise or detailed vision. Thus, the range for professional choice is smaller, further limiting their future life perspective.

Based on the interview with the mother and the son DV, it was concluded that the main reason for the low rate of visually impaired people in Universities comes from the school base, that is, lack of incentives often from the family itself, financial difficulties to buy the necessary equipment (glasses, magnifiers, image amplifiers, among others) and many schools still do not offer all the support for inclusion.

Although at a slow pace, Brazil has managed to increase the inclusion of students with disabilities in the education system. In 2017, the number of enrolments of this group in basic education was 827,243. The previous year it was 751,065. The index has been growing for four consecutive years. However, despite this, the structure of schools is still insufficient to cater for this population (AUMENTA, 2018).

According to data from the 2017 Basic Education School Census, released by the Ministry of Education (MEC), the rate of inclusion of people with disabilities in regular classes, which is recommended, increased from 85.5% in 2013 to 90.9% in 2017. Most students with disabilities, however, do not have access to specialised educational care. Only 40.1% manage to use the service.

Compared to 2013, secondary education managed to almost double the number of enrolments of people with disabilities, from 48,589 to 94,274 in 2017. But this group still corresponds to a derisory percentage of the total enrolment in the stage, only 1.2%.

In primary education, the percentage of enrolments of pupils with disabilities in relation to the total is 2.8 per cent, a higher rate than in secondary education, but the rate of growth has been slower and the capacity to cater for this group is even lower, with only 29.8 per cent of schools having adequate facilities for this public.

The structure is not only deficient in adaptations for students with disabilities. Among municipal schools, which account for 71.5% of all early childhood education institutions, only 29.7% have a library or reading room.

Thus, the credibility of the blind themselves to graduate is low, so that they do not even have the will to continue. There is a lack of facility, encouragement and support.

3.3 HOW TO STRUCTURE THE LIBRARY

3.3.1 OPTICAL RESOURCESNON-OPTICAL RESOURCES

Optical aids or resources are special-purpose lenses or a device consisting of a set of lenses, usually of high power, with the aim of magnifying the retinal image. It should be remembered that the use of lenses, magnifiers, spectacles, telescopes represents a valuable gain in terms of quality, comfort and visual performance for near vision, but does not rule out the need for material adaptation and other care. Thus, the use of optical and non-optical resources is important for the reading of the disabled, and some of this equipment should be made available for use in libraries.

Optical features include:
- Hand-held magnifiers or table and stand magnifiers: useful for enlarging the size of fonts for reading, the dimensions of maps, graphs, diagrams, figures, etc. The larger the magnification, the smaller the field of vision with a decrease in reading speed and greater visual fatigue.

Among the non-optical ones, we have:
- Enlarged type: enlargement of fonts, signs and graphic symbols in books, handouts, single texts, games, diaries, among others.
- Yellow acetate: reduces the incidence of glare on the paper.

Fig 10- Yellow cellophane. Source: FCM/Unicamp.

- Inclined plane: adapted desk, with the table inclined so that the student can carry out the activities with visual comfort and stability of the spine.
- Accessories: 4B or 6B pencils, porous-tipped pens, bookends, notebooks with spaced black staves, typescopes (reading guide), tape recorders.
- Software with screen magnifiers and programmes with speech synthesis.
- Books and handouts in Braille
- Closed circuit television - CCTV: a device attached to a monochrome or colour TV monitor that magnifies images up to 60 times and transfers them to the monitor.

Fig 12- Visually impaired student at Roberto Clarck uses the CCTV. Source: Folha da Região On-line[2].

3.1.1 . PHYSICAL SPACE AND FURNITURE

The global perception of space is given by the various zones that, related by function, proximity or circulation, make up the building. Circulation, as a linear architectural element and organiser of the whole, is the main element that gives clarity to the environment. In the same way, large spaces, such as a courtyard or meeting points, give off clarity.

As for the delimitation of space, it is clear that visually impaired people understand its geometric form. In the case of the blind, vertical planes such as walls and ramparts, when grouped together, acquire a form with specific functions, characterising a given environment in the same way that the delimitation is perceived in mental drawings, through horizontal lines on paper. The presence of openings does not weaken the sense of closure of the space, and the form remains intact and perceptible (MOSCHETTA, 2007).

It can be seen that the legibility of the built environment, from the perspective of the visually impaired, is provided by the simplifications of spatial organisation and geometric form, in the same way that the presence of linear architectural elements such as circulation are important to understanding the relationship between the various environments of the building.

In addition, the presence of four vertical planes delimiting the space has an important impact on the perception of visually impaired people. In principle, it is understood that the simpler the geometric form and the structure of architectural composition, the more legible the building will be for them. In this way, circulation as part of the architectural design is an important element for understanding and articulation between the various environments. On the contrary, isolated blocks make it difficult to understand the whole. Above all, it is important to recognise the architectural elements most easily perceived by the disabled from their spatial experiences (MOSCHETTA, 2007).

It should be remembered that the configuration of physical space is not immediately perceived by blind pupils, as it is by those who can see. Therefore, it is necessary to

enable knowledge and recognition of the physical space and furniture layout. The collection of information will take place in a procedural and analytical way through the exploration of the concrete space of the environment, in this case the library.

Thus, we can emphasise that: doors should be left fully open or closed to avoid unpleasant surprises or accidents; furniture should be stable and any changes should be notified. It is advisable to reserve a space in the library with suitable furniture for the arrangement of the instruments used by these pupils who must take care of the order and organisation of the material in order to assimilate useful points of reference for them.

CHAPTER 4

RESULTS AND FINAL CONSIDERATIONS

Based on the understanding of the *wayfinding*, graphic space and environmental design approach, in which some authors, such as Bins Ely, Lynch, Scariot, Passini, Siegel and White, have highlighted the main elements: paths/circulation; *landmarks;* nodes; boundaries; zones/districts; routes; and configuration; we have that the Library structure must count, at least with these.

In reference to the Library of UNESP of Bauru we have that, the access is not limited by the structure of the library itself, but of the whole university building, in which it does not present facilities for the access of any physical disabled. Emphasising the visually impaired, the structure of the classrooms, the cafeteria or any other public space for social coexistence, is not adapted according to the main elements.

The cognitive map of each person needs tactile and auditory landmarks to be formed. However, although the UNESP Library has reading equipment and resources, tactile floors and maps, there is not enough signalling inside the entire structure, and this is limited only from the library entrance to the aids (computers, scanners, Braille books). That is, the rest of the path/space from the library to the other books, tables, study rooms and secretariat is limited and restricted to people with VI.

Much of this lack of attention, for inclusion and support within the university as a whole, comes from the lack of visually impaired students in the student space itself, since primary school, worsening over the other years. Thus, there are no financial incentives prioritised and/or earmarked for the adequacy of university space for the disabled, both physical and visual.

In addition, all the other essential elements for the *wayfinding* process are only possible for users with normal vision, where zones, routes and nodes are configured by visual points of differentiation of the environment and / or opening of passage, which are not so easy for people with disabilities to identify.

Therefore, knowing that it is a right, socially speaking, that any citizen of the world has access to public space, a change of incentives from the base of education must be kept in mind, so that inclusion, especially in schools, universities and other learning environments, is effective. In the case of UNESP, there is a need to expand tactile, sound, lighting and visual artefacts throughout all buildings, not only in all buildings, not just in a small limited space, so that it enables the spatial orientation of an entire universe.

Fig 13- Facade of the UNESP Bauru Library. Source: Alumni Unesp

CHAPTER 5

REFERENCES

ADG **Associação dos Designers Gráficos** (Brazil). ABC da ADG: glossary of terms and entries used in graphic design. São Paulo: ADG, 2000

ALMEIDA, M.F.X.M. **Auxílios À navegação de pedestres cegos através de mapas táteis**. 2008. Dissertation (Master in Design - Postgraduate programme in Design, UFPE, Recife.

AMARAL, l. **Stories of exclusion: and inclusion? - in public schools.** In: CONSELHOREGIONALDEPSICÓLOGOS.EducaçãoEspecial em debate. SP: Casado Psicólogo/Conselho Regional de Psicologia, 1997, p 23-34. Conhecendo a deficiência. SP: Robe, 1995

Increasing Inclusion of Students with Disabilities, but Schools Have No Structure ToReceive Them. **O Globo**, 31 Jan. 2018. Available at: <https://oglobo.globo.com/sociedade/educacao/aumenta-inclusao-de-alunos-com- disability-but-schools-do-not-have-the-structure-to-receive-them-22348736> Accessed: 18 Dec. 2018

BEDROSSIAN, Rebecca. Environmental Graphic Design. Communication Arts. March/April 2008. page 84/102.

BINS ELY, V. H. M.; DISCHINGER, M.; MATTOS, M. L. **Environmental information systems - indispensable elements for accessibility and orientability.** Brazilian Congress of Ergonomics, XII; Latin American Congress of Ergonomics, VII; Brazilian Seminar of Integral Accessibility, I, 2002, Recife. **Annals....** Recife: ABERGO, 2002.

BRASIL. Law n. 9.394, of 20 December 1996. **MEC Portal**. Establishes the guidelines and bases of national education. Brasília, 1996. Available at: < http://portal.mec.gov.br/seesp/index.php?option=content&task=view&id=159&Itemid= 311>. Accessed on: 15 July 2016.

BRAZIL. Ministry of Education. **Secretariat of Special Education.** Portaria n. 1.010, dellde May 2006. Available at: <http://www.universia.com.br/html/noticia/ noticia_dentrodocampus_cjfcg.html> Accessed on: 05 dejul. 2007.

BRAZIL. Ministry of Education. **Secretariat of Fundamental Education**. Parâmetros

CurricularesNacionais: curricular adaptations. Brasília, 1998.

COSTA, Jane A. **Adapting for low vision**. Brasília: MEC, SEESP, 2000.

DISCHINGER, M. **Designing for all senses: accessible spaces for visually impaired citizens**, Goteborg, Chalmers University of Technology, 2000.

FERREIRA, Abrahão Lincoln. "NetSaber - Articles." **Cartoons and Ideology In the Second World War**, artigos.netsaber.com.br/resumo_artigo_24079/artigo_sobre_aplicacao-do-design- gráfico-na-elaboracao-de-projetos-that-facilitate-a-vida-do-deficiente-visual.

FERREIRA, Elise M. B. [Monografia], **Recursos Didáticos -** uma possibilidade de produzir conhecimentos^. UNIRIO, Rio de Janeiro/RJ, 1998.

FERRONATO, R. **A construção de instrumento de inclusão no ensino da Matemática.** 2002. Dissertation (Master in Production Engineering). Federal University of Santa Catarina, Florianópolis, 2002.

GIBSON, D. **The Wayfinding Handbook**: Information Design for Public Places. Princeton. Architectural Press, 2009.

GIBSON, James. **The ecological approach to visual perception**. Boston: Houghton Miffin, 1986.

HARON, S.N.; HAMID, M. Y; TALIB, A. **Towards Healthcare Service Quality:** An Understanding of the Usability Concept in Healthcare Design. In: Procedia - Social and Behavioral Sciences, v.42, p.63-73, 2012.

HENRIQUES A.; ATTIE J. P.; FARIAS L. M. S. **Theoretical references of French didactics: didactic analysis aiming at the study of multiple integrals with the aid of Maple software**. Educação MatemáticaPesquisa, v. 9, n.1, p.51-81, 2007.

HUNT, Wayne. **Environmental Graphics**: Projects & Process. New York: Harper Collins, 2003.

ISTOMIN, K. V.; DWYER, M. J. A. **Critical Discussion of Anthropological Theories of Human Spatial Orientation with Reference to Reindeer Herders of Northeastern Europe and Western Siberia.** In: Current Anthropology, v.50, n° 01, NY, USA. 2009

JACOB, Eduardo Louis. **Environmental Graphics: typicals and topics**. 2007. Dissertation (master's degree). São Paulo - Pontifical Catholic University of São Paulo, Postgraduate Studies Programme in Communication and Semiotics.

JACOBSON, A. **Health-care facilities.** In: BERGER, C. Wayfinding: Designing and Implementing GraphicNavigational Systems. Rotovision Switzerland. p.84-97. 2009.

LANDAUER, T.K. **The trouble with computers: Usefulness, usability and productivity.** Cambridge, MA: MIT Press. 1995.

LARAMARA - Brazilian Association for Assistance to the Visually Impaired. Contact Magazine. **Conversations about Visual Deficiency**, year 3, nª 5, p. 33-44, May, 1993.

LIMA, F.J. **Predicting barriers, anticipating solutions, avoiding accidents.** Description of the research project Education -Programme 25001019001P-7Educação, UFPE, 2004.
Mental Representation of Tactile Stimuli. Ribeirão Preto, 1998.166p. Dissertation (Master). Faculty of Philosophy, Sciences and Letters of Ribeirão Preto, University of São Paulo, 1998.

LYNCH, K. **The Image of the City**. São Paulo: Martins Fontes, 1999.

MAZZOTA, M. **Educação Especial no Brasil: história e políticas públicas.** SP: Cortez, 1996. Teaching work and training of teachers of Special Education. SP: EPU, 1993.

MEC, SEESP, 2005. MEC. Secretariat of Special Education. **Training Programme for Human Resources in Primary Education, Visual Impairment**, vol.2, 2001.

MINISTRY OF EDUCATION. **Knowledge and practices of inclusion: communication and signalling difficulties: physical disability.** Brasília: MEC, 2004.

MOSCHETTA, Vanessa Carla, and Gislaine Elizete BELOTO. "**SPACIAL LIVES AND THE PERCEPTION OF PLACE BY DISABLED PEOPLE.**" *Revista Tecnológica*, 2007, periodicos.uem.br/ojs/index.php/RevTecnol/article/viewFile/4991/4208.

MRECH, LENY MAGALHÃES - **THE MAIN PARADIGMS OF SPECIAL EDUCATION** - paper presented in Natal, March 1999.

MRECH, LENY MAGALHÃES - **PSICANÁLISE E EDUCAÇÃO: NOVOS OPERADORES DE LEITURA.** São Paulo, Editora Pioneira, 1999

MRECH, L.**What is inclusive education?** Revista Integração. MEC:Brasília, v. 8, n.20, p. 37-39, 1998.

OLIVEIRA, Regina C. S.; Newton Kara-José e Marcos W.S. **Entendendo a Baixa Visão: orientações aos professores**. MEC, SEESP, 2000.

PADOVANI, S.; MOURA, D. **Navigation in Hypermedia: A user-centred approach**. Rio de Janeiro. Ed. CiênciaModerna. 2008.

PASSINI, R.; PROULX, G. **Wayfinding without vision: an experiment withcongenitally totally blind people**. Environment and Behavior, v. 20, p. 227,1988.

Available at:<http://eab.sagepub.com/cgi/content/abstract/20/2/277>. Accessed on: 29 Dec. 2015.

PEIXOTO, J. L. B.; SANTANA, E. R. dos S.; CAZORLA, I. M. **Soroban: a tool for understanding the four operations.** Itabuna: Via Litterarum, 2006.

RABARDEL, P. **Les hommes et les technologies: approche cognitive des Instruments contemporains.** Paris: Armand Colin, 1995.

RABARDEL, P. **Qu'est-ce qu'un instrument ? Appropriation, conceptualisation, mises en situation.** In: Outils pour le calcul et le traçage de courbes CNDP-DIE - mar. 1995. Available at: <http://www.cndp.fr/archivage/valid/13420-1126-1194.pdf.>. Accessed on: 10 March 2016.

RANGEL, M. M. **Colour and Ergonomics of the Built Environment: an investigation of spatial orientation in a hospital environment.** Dissertation (master) - Pontifical Catholic University of Rio de Janeiro, Department of Arts and Design. 2011.

RAUBAL, M., et al. **Structuring Space with Image Schemata: Wayfinding in Airports as a Case Study**. In: Proceedings of the International Conference on Spatial Information Theory. 1997. Available at: Accessed on: mar. 2016

ROSA, Alberto; OCHAÍTA, **Esperanza. Psychology of Blindness.** Alianza Editorial S.A. Madrid, 1993.

SANTIN, Sílvya; SIMMONS JoyceNester. **Blind Children with Congenital Visual Impairment**. Revista Benjamin Constant, nª 2,January, 1996.

SASSAKI,R. Special interview for Revista Integração. Integration Magazine. MEC:Brasília,v.8, n. 20, p.09-17, 1998.

SCARIOT, C. A. **Evaluation of information systems for Wayfinding: a comparative study** between Academy and market in Curitiba. 2013. Dissertation (master's degree in

Design - Postgraduate Programme in Information Systems Design, Federal University of Paraná, Curitiba.

SIEGEL, A. W.; WHITE, S. H. **The development of spatial representations oflarge- scale environments.** In Reese, H. W. (Ed.), Advances in Child Development and Behavior, v. 10: 9-55. Academic Press, London. 1975.

UNGAR, S. **Cognitive mappingwithoutvisual experience**. In: KITCHIN, R.;FREUNDSCHUH, S. (Ed.) **Cognitive mapping: past, present and future**. London: Routledge, 2000. p.221-248. Available at:<http://www.psy.surrey.ac.uk/staff/SUngar.htm>. Accessed on: 9 Jan. 2016.

VERILLON, P. **La problématique de Penseignement: un cadre pour penser Penseignement du graphisme.** Revue GRAF & TEC. v. 0, n. 0, 1996.

ANNEX 1 - DATA FROM THE NGO AVISTAR

The NGO Avistar is a non-profit organisation that aims to promote favourable conditions for the full development of people with visual impairment, ensuring their socio-educational-cultural integration, their professional insertion and their quality of life.

Avista's users are people who, despite their visual impairment, seek their place in society and make every effort to overcome obstacles.

Mission: to promote favourable conditions for the integral development of the visually impaired person, through projects that promote their social inclusion, respecting individual and social needs.

Vision: To promote the integration of the visually impaired person and their family into society, through projects that meet their needs, such as habilitation/rehabilitation, professional training and also projects aimed at leisure and culture.

Access link: http://avistar.org.br/nossos-projetos/

I want morebooks!

Buy your books fast and straightforward online - at one of world's fastest growing online book stores! Environmentally sound due to Print-on-Demand technologies.

Buy your books online at
www.morebooks.shop

Kaufen Sie Ihre Bücher schnell und unkompliziert online – auf einer der am schnellsten wachsenden Buchhandelsplattformen weltweit! Dank Print-On-Demand umwelt- und ressourcenschonend produziert.

Bücher schneller online kaufen
www.morebooks.shop

info@omniscriptum.com
www.omniscriptum.com

www.ingramcontent.com/pod-product-compliance
Lightning Source LLC
Chambersburg PA
CBHW022016300426
44117CB00005B/225